DRANK, RECRUITED

FIRST POETS SERIES 24

ONTARIO ARTS COUNCIL
CONSEIL DES ARTS DE L'ONTARIO

an Ontario government agency
un organisme du gouvernement de l'Ontario

Canada Council   Conseil des arts
for the Arts   du Canada

Guernica Editions Inc. acknowledges the support of
the Canada Council for the Arts and the Ontario Arts Council.
The Ontario Arts Council is an agency of the Government of Ontario.

We acknowledge the financial support of the Government of Canada.

AMI XHERRO

DRANK, RECRUITED

GUERNICA
EDITIONS

TORONTO • CHICAGO • BUFFALO • LANCASTER (U.K.)
2023

Guernica Founder: Antonio D'Alfonso

Michael Mirolla, general editor
Elana Wolff, editor
Cover, interior design: Rafael Chimicatti
Guernica Editions Inc.
287 Templemead Drive, Hamilton, ON L8W 2W4
2250 Military Road, Tonawanda, N.Y. 14150-6000 U.S.A.
www.guernicaeditions.com

Distributors:
Independent Publishers Group (IPG)
600 North Pulaski Road, Chicago IL 60624
University of Toronto Press Distribution (UTP)
5201 Dufferin Street, Toronto (ON), Canada M3H 5T8

First edition.
Printed in Canada.

Legal Deposit—Third Quarter
Library of Congress Catalog Card Number: 2022952287
Library and Archives Canada Cataloguing in Publication
Title: Drank, recruited / Ami Xherro.
Names: Xherro, Ami, author.
Series: First poets series (Toronto, Ont.) ; 24.
Description: Series statement: First poets series ; 24
Identifiers: Canadiana 20220498547 | ISBN 9781771838245 (softcover)
Classification: LCC PS8646.H44 D73 2023 | DDC C811/.6—dc23

Loveliest of what I leave behind is the sunlight,
and loveliest after that the shining stars, and the moon's face,
but also cucumbers that are ripe, and pears, and apples.
　　　　—Praxilla of Sicyon

I'm the loneliest soul in this deserted grove!
Wandering further then, I realize:
If I really want to deliver myself from you,
I'll need to live outside myself. It's true.
Or else you will have to move further from my eyes.
　　　　　—Louise Labé, "I Run from Town and Temple"

CONTENTS

How to pronounce my name, 9

Come closer, 10

The tap, 11

Body is a bridge to July, 13

Come man come, 15

Swimmer, 18

Writers at the writer's workshop on "Swimmer", 20

Full moon, 22

Letter to Dynamo, 23

Image, 25

Rooms for life, 27

Things the body remembered when I stood against the wind, 29

The cocktail party, 41

Feeling, 43

Method of meditation, 45

Exobiography, 47

Woods, 52

You, 54

The thumb, 55

The big toe, 56

Hesitate to call, 58

The inauguration of nasty, 60

In a day, 62

[DAYS], 66

Aphorisms in that fact, 70

Stamps no one can rip off my flesh, 73

The end, 75

If I'm flesh then you're that other part, 76

To existing so stone, 78

To birds at the end of his adolescence, 79
Nothing goes into the dark trees to vanish, 81
I want to want you, 82
Neighbours, 84
I could have had a better time, 85
Institutes, 87
March 1998, 89
Two photographs, 90
Visiting, 95
Unavoidably yours, 98
Outside your door, 99
Let's, 101

Notes, 102
Acknowledgements, 103
About the Author, 104

How to pronounce my name

A deaf sky over the crumbled earth

ripped out my clothes, feverish
my throat
gagged with dust.

In the dirt I cling to myself.

Come closer

I want to forget words today
Let looks speak for themselves
Let the trembling hand speak
of this tried-at life

Middled like Brazil
Slovakia-hung

Sun–the proportions of which
man and man comprehend
slicing the billiards table
with their scent

Good is impossible to wear

Though your jacket is world peace
Your mouth clean blitz

The tap

If I live
or lived
as I live
or do
let me in
let me get to know you

who to ask
who to pass

through whom does it last

not to hear one's echo in the world

no to finding a twin
no to the grinning bowl
nor the shining spoon

as much listening as required
more

I came here to speak more of less
now I cover myself with the cloth
of my dying breath

who can speak to me of this

who knows what of their knowing
intending to pick up an object
and put it back

the tap drips

having served you
it will say:

I have known your need

I have known devotion
to your motherless palm

Body is a bridge to July

Lusted after. Hurry curl.
Woolenweep. Love forever
if you recall.
Surrender.
A night walk,
a billowed bawl
of wet tasty island tears.

You leopard you,
pull your pants
down beside the bed,
take your nearness to lower cause,
your naked to open shores.

Jasper-tongued
vowels to bedroom window—
Out! out! out!

Bare is the night.
Our birthplace broke our hearts.

I need your body
but there is none—
only a vision for trying.

I need your body
crowded with itself.

O the quiet spread
all-surrounding,
breaks the night in two.

Come man come

Hello
from the haunch.
Summer's touch stinks like a shrine.
Wading forth an axe:
Failing flower, given son.

I am nearby
attending blindly to your ally,
whiskey.

You have been known to mourn,
so I tell a lie.

My underwear between
two parted lips:
I make your scene,
I lose my poison.

Let come whoever is cool,
I am on his side.
Let him come.
Slight rain spilt
from the devil's grip,
I was your girl for a week.

The prize you played so well:
golden letters in morning's bust,
My hero: string across and die.

                    Should you receive in my flesh
                    the moon's scorn,
                    I take my final kiss
                    from your belt.

Wheeling out blue lines,
swimming,
then cigarette.

Bent over the shore,
coming down bare
on a fat woman's shadow.
I did not die like I wanted—
laughing at flowers,
waiting by the door.

We never played from a distance.
I wanted only the exploits of danger
over you, my rank volcano,
singing like a crowded chore

through a whale's gorge
and water swells when you dance,
junkyard sirens blow you at dawn.

Your sanity cannot
be comforted with kisses.
The asthmatic wages
gambled by your ancestors
cannot be won again.

My heart is for passing
through.
Men reach land
squinting through Captain's pockets.

My heart is for losing
to mine eyes,
for there are ugly walls
enough,
and ugly men.

Swimmer

I saw you jump into water,
where day ends
                        wrapped like a gift

floozy sun in your pants.

I half believe you will leave me for land
dying word's *flue* because swimming
shoulders where breath ends
eyes busy, yawning
                        over purple horizon
                                    sliced eggplant—
                                            half-skin
                                                    allies

floating with your back on the water.

I like you mild
I like me milder,
two waltzing bees in saltwater

fugued from a capless bottle.

Lovemaking with the dignity of walking
talking with free excitement,
reeling in your sun
like a gooseberry.

My swimmer farthest from shore
has something to say
but is embarrassed to say it.
A laugh lays down
the horizon
flat

l'aurore aux sandales d'or

Dusk rides
his own yawn.
I aim inside the golden belt

where dark eyes saunter   accents falter

from where you meet   they go   not follow

Coal for killers
    Ash for empires
        Gem dealers
            There a king without features

[   ]
Not worse to be brief:
convince fire
to drink water

Writers at the writer's workshop on "Swimmer"

It's about love in water, sex and passion,
reminds me of what my mother said:
sex is like fire and it's a woman's job to keep it under control.
Surreal things like that.
To me, it's an expanded reality.
I didn't say distorted, I said expanded.
When I see something like that it always comes to the
surface again,
it can change every time I read it.
With that inside I can change it because it changes you.
Straightforward poetry it comes and it goes.
I'm not saying it should be that way.
This is the first time I sit with people,
the first time I read what I felt.
When I go from Longfellow to Browning—
need to wrap my mind around it,
not to drastically cohere to a frame.
Actually, I have my own issues with surrealism.
I desired to be led a little more,
as simple as who is talking to who.
I thought I might want to rearrange your words,
strike the chord I want to.
The imagery demands a lot—
I mean the images are beautiful but I want something
to connect the saltshaker blues with the hot dog and the
slender man—
its structure more than its content.

I mean Jackson Pollock and the splashing of things—
not to make a noise but a splash.
I did find my quote—"As beautiful as the chance encounter
between …"
It seems to me the poem might be about the anxiety of
separation
or love changing.
It seems to me there is a lot going on—just a little more
clarification.
It's sort of heartbreaking to read.

Full moon

No one who is truly dying is aware of it.
They wanted to put this guy in a straitjacket
but first they put leeches on his torso
and locked him up in a windowless room
to cure him of any remaining paranoia.

Fear is unique to the living.
Even the possibility of death
cannot tire us of eternity
and its accidental grace.

Letter to Dynamo

I try passing through feeling, laughing, and playing.

I read poems about cows in fields, the teeth of dogs,
adolescent anecdotes turning condolence into doctrine.

I wear a costume, misdial, laugh, adore my own fun, ask
about you, humanity, response, abstract this willingness,
appreciate the tip, get soft, paw at misgivings, ask how you
are like a scared mistress on the other end of a landline,
succeed in devotion and tell you too.

To phone you is a tactless coax to persuade the too-forgotten
deliciousness of those kisses, to remind you of like desires
expressed through like bodies.

You forgot my breasts, and parts you do not have. My body
is a house for winter, for quick scenes, slow exits. Now I do,
now I linger. Now I delay.

Apricots line the windowsill and birds are too tired for
carnage. Now I do. Now I remember your indecisive hair, a
charade for genius, and your cheery strut in too-short pants.

I have imitation fun with my bed and breakfast. I
remember butter and bread but how to discern providence
from your appetite?

A person is a small company of strangers. Against-you eyes bride my heart.

Unpool your loving: I gave it free. I gave it from my mouth like a jaundiced libertine. I gave it rigged with vision and honey for its load.

Slender maverick, lover of figs, outgrow your name and cry for me!

Now I do remember the hourshore slumber and the protocol of sleep: your face is just as clever under half-whetted light.

Everything pardons you with deference. Your beige is easy and good.

Image

Am I alone here?
Am I the only
masturbator
on this page?
Did you
or did you not
jerk to
your white
fleeting
gods
earlier today,
reading
the paper?
You're sorry,
I know what
you do
when you're
all alone.
You know
what I would do
to find a warm thing
to be caught in.

Anyway
I wanted to know
if I was alone here.
I wanted a Really
Big Romance.

To clear the image
from my eye,
It will take a breath
It will take a truck
It will take a China
It will take a Valium
It will take the endurance of a family's bickering
It will take the language of love
for desire to exit
for something to take its place.

Rooms for life

How are you doing?
I'm a loose flare
licking its wound
is how I'm doing.

I'm in Life,
the largest room in the world.
Here is the window
that leads what's out
to what's out back.

Here is my desk.
The walls muffle my pulse

                              dank—dank

Try to do nothing here.
Try to do something.
Arrive without bags,
it makes you buoyant.

In Life's afterlife, life
wears Life's distant look

at my desk

                              dig—dig—dig

Sumerians buried their dead
with their things.

All things led
across time.
Chairs drag the floor,

white meets bone,
infirm
low light—

television on.

Yawn—that changeless business
fills me with Arrogant Treasure

ching-ching

Things the body remembered
when I stood against the wind

1

tak-tak-tak
footsteps

tak-tak
foot
steps

cat steps
in snow

in the garden,
cat walks
on snow

one watches,
one goes

2

2 pm
the glass to my right
brims shallow
light because it knows me

2 eyes can be found there
swimming with a banana peel

this is effortless
community,

web
of unhurried
predators

sits on a beach,
wish I could join

but I am their god,
they don't feel me.

3

I thought I liked you

I thought I liked you

when I first saw you

I see now

you're

nothing but

nothing but

a rubber prince

bubber prince.

You fool me a little.

What's the price of smoke?

4

YOU ATE TOO MUCH

YOU ATE TOO MUCH

YOU JUST ATE TOO MUCH

YOU ARE FEELING THAT FEELING OF EATING TOO
MUCH

YOU ATE TOO MANY CHIPS

ATE TOO MANY KINDER BUENO MINIS

AFTER YOU HAD A GLASS OF WINE

YOU ATE TOO MUCH

5

In a small universe:
no adequate lovers,
only incomplete loves.

Two buttons remain by virtuosity,
and a Coca Cola can by sheer luck.

6

Do not make yourself uncertain
or ask the swarm for answers.
Rats and ribbons cling to
the cloudless burden of being.

7

The beating sun is faintly heard
amid the echoes of its cage—

in my purse—
the muffled coins

8

L   AST   N   IGH   T

I W   AS   TH   INK   ING

OF   A   B   ELT   A

V   ER   Y   W   ELL   W

TH   ICK   L   EATH   ER

TH   AT   IS   UH   SO   W

IT   UH   H   ANGS   PER

ON   B   OTH   E   ND S

ORN

B   ELT

ORN   IN   TH   AT

FEC   TL   Y   F   LAT

OF   TH   E   N   AI   L

9

When I eat   everything expands.

Sleep   there are scenes.

Speak   there are things.

10 / Song for the dentist's office

cumquats

cum squats

carom tarts

come lots

11

It is enjoyable to enjoy things
and enjoyable to not enjoy them.

The cocktail party

I am wrapped in the most unchanging fabric.
People like Randy can't get it.
They suicide.
It would be sad if time stayed put.
But it doesn't.
I am at cocktail hour with death.
The artists are here.
So are the donors.
They say *artists are so fake.*
Nod. Nod. Applause.
Artists are as fake
as zippers. As false
as change,
the robe itself.
Donors want snow.
Hail. Hail.
They want an avalanche.
Beds. Beds.
Everything changes for no one.
You can call the 20th century
though it's occupied.
Listen.
A little lamp heats the space.
I hate the word hearth.
I hate nothing.
I'm wrapped in a fabric
so tight
I can smell my breath.
The wind sermonizes.

The spritz are drunk.
The fizz famed for its
'obliviousness
enters me,
and I forget I'm fake.
Randy is the artist
I pay to sing.
I cry.
Everything is beautiful.
Time tears at the edges of its forgotten invitation.
I am happy.
Randy gave up art
to build this city.
Now he sings.

Feeling

Your parents
named you
what they
wanted.

It's not your job
to sit here
meaning
to mean
or feeling
to feel.

You could be really feeling it boys,
walking around shaking it in our faces.
You could be putting it
right in front of us,

with the good feeling
of being
and being
right to be.

Your paradise
is full of feeling
and your friends' feelings

and my paradise
is full of feeling
too.

Paradise is a hell
of feeling,

In care of meaning
there's a paradise
of feeling
which is hell
to let go.

Method of meditation

Have I laugh tube
Have I foot laughter

Have I style demand
Have I ambition
to be useless

Have I humility
to be fun

Have I erection
in memory
Have I invitation

Have I meaning
to be contradicted
Have I error in me

Am I body
doing body
in the obscurity of its system

Who will love
my small within
containing—

Who will love
my infinite without—

Who, handforced,
leaves the possible
to who loves it,

Who loves to be polite

Who runs to her rest stop
Who blazes into the tomb

Who halves bread with thought
Who remains unbought

Exobiography

I have consumed terrible things.
I have seen things that possessed me.
I was a name in that revelation.
I did my work without understanding.
I worked where I rested.
I rested where I fucked.

We went to the clinic after the bar
to unhave my baby.
In both you said, *Drink this.*

I drank once for the want of it,
twice to be rid of it.

I drank the first time because I was afraid to drink the second time.
I drank the first time to prepare myself to drink the second time.
I drank the first time so I had to drink less the second time.
I drank the first time without knowing so the second was my
    first time.
I drank once because I wanted, twice because I needed it to die.
I drank once to be recruited, twice to recruit others.
I drank the first time so it was easier to drink the second time.
I drank once because I wanted, twice for the memory.

I drank November like a nail wrapped in lycra.
I swallowed December then January in splintered rage.
I swallowed March in burlap,
finally the April rain, which made my soul

wet and heavy and—
my god hurt I,
my god.

Had I the frankest possible discussion with myself,
had I seen that look in mine eyes,
I would have died
in life
in art
in time.

You ate a hamburger while they sucked me,
formally.
I had apple juice,
dreamt fossils
along my spine, gave
looks of love
in Alexander's tomb
and rode death home.
I rode the train,
moody for the fame,
for the doomed heart of
a drugged woman,
near-died.
Still men live
having died.

For the impeached dream—
Cream Cream Cream!
I did it.
I did it.
I had been known to do it,
tit-lipped and pussyruined.

Now the wisdom-cyst grows in me.
I glean the source by drink.
I keep you in my fridge
so when you ask for a beer I can say
I loved you a little,
Miller,
The heart blinds itself a little.

Making a baby
on adult furniture,

Making the thing
by lampshade,

Making the thing
snugly—

In that universal yawn
I made the thing
commonly
as I did

against the lovesheath
of my slutbatter,
better than butter
better than butter.

Let the making
Let you
Let baby
be anything to me
before
I am implicated
into
any
archetype
for wanting to
roll in the sun.

Though nature is green it should be red
for what it makes women do.

I take your hot sun
into the hole of my face.
Hell hems the earth—

AH I YELL I YELL I AM YELLING I AM NOT
JUMPING OUT OF MY CHAIR I AM CERTAINLY
FROTHING WITH THIS FAILING VOICE FAILING
WITH THE BANALITY OF VIOLENCE OF A WOMAN

SILENTLY YELLING INTO A SCREEN SCREAMING
AND SILENTLY

HERE I AM YELLING AGAIN I NEED A GLASS
OF WATER I WANT A SNACK I WANT A BLOW
JOB I WANT TO GIVE A BLOW JOB I WANT TO BE
TRANSFORMED INTO A SEXY OUTFIT I WANT
ANOTHER LOVER I WANT TO SEE WHAT SUMER
WAS LIKE I WANT TO GO TO APOLLONIA TO
MEET MY MOTHER

Now I write our autobiography
which
is reductive,
imitative,
is a translation.

It reads:

1. DID NOT BUY MEAT FROM THE BAKERY
2. DID NOT PEE AT CAFÉ LE ROI
3. ALL THE LIGHTS OF CORFU LOOK LIKE TEARY
   EYES

Woods

1

Sick
Ordinary
Unlocalizable Toilet
All A Toilet
Humming the Vertigo of the Centre
Feminine Wipes for Prudence
Righteousness
Woodly Nobility
Embarkedly Royal
Engreening itself with Language
Spineless Noon
The Bluetooth Sounds of
Daddy Cool

2

Name these places between clouds
all measured by distance from the other.
Around others we survey our eye contact.
I smile behind teeth.
Name those places in the mouth where orange, red, blue meet.
Name those words so plainly spoken that give name
to that feeling of being ordinarily taken up
behind which the eyes cower with certainty
of having been seen as they might,
beyond the blackness beyond

beyond an insurmountable beyond
behind where spruces stand—couples at
a dance when the music stops suddenly—
through which the wind makes
the moss whisper—
Do not offer me a world
if I can't be a dream.

3

The beetled morning slumps over my tent.
Laughter warms the outer edges of the fire
cricketing beyond the voices which reach it.
Aerosol, oil intent on insolence
entertains, annoys, tempts
the flying nuisances
who are victorious in most aspects.

Voices of people I almost know speckle the sunset—
fetters of seagull and sky.
I bring 4 books 2 notebooks 3 pencils and a sharpener.
I turn underwear inside out.
I shiver with rocks.
I think repetition in films is impossible
the way you can read a sentence over and over in a book:

I had been ready for anything. But not for the kettle.
One must understand what the drop is
that makes the kettle overflow.

You

angel face
clever chested
shoreless
sandbagged
nameless
turned up loud
what you keep inside
what I would to climb
handslice that sky
penalty sleeper
slanted fuck
how earth flickered shut
aching for you

The thumb

is obvious

except for the part of the glove also called 'the thumb.'

To press into a socket,

except for a lift cross-river.

Also the fattest finger,

except when measuring rum in a glass.

Still less obvious than

the lingerer.

The porch of your hand,

the thumb.

The big toe

Keeps us attached
so hum the golden jelly
from bottom to top.
Timetube
without memory
tick ticks
with invitation,
the test erection.

I am all clock
in meditation.
I am all
lazy
in life, except
sleep: highest order
of human activity.

Fish don't sleep.
Frogs don't sleep.
Flies sleep
though their lives
are indiscernible from it.

I am wholly sleeping
when I am doing
the things I do
in the service of my being.

What is not sleep,
what is not
aliveness enough
to beat the world
out of us.

Hesitate to call

Love is not enough you said certainly.
Ducks overcome me,
eating grass which is all the world
and I no matter how badly want you—

So this is what it is—
You are working at home.
I had to leave to not be overcome with leaving.
I had to be with ducks in a storm.

Last night in a dream
my fascism was tested by a man who
wanted to buy me.

He asked whether communists climb
lighthouses.
This was a trick.
People climb lighthouses.

While waiting for the rain
I wrote I needed to be
optimistic but how can I be optimistic
when it's clear you don't want me.

Enthusiasm on the other hand
is to have the gods in you
where they have left
the door slightly ajar.

How agape is enough,
Is open the plenty
of love,
How miserable
forgiveness
served thus.

I had to be the malignant one,
the bad darling.
I had to be the alliance of the door
with the hallway.
I had to be the fish fry smell
wafting corridors,
ushering out onto the street.
I had to soonly leave.

I numbed going
with the mouth,
the hands,
the imprecise vocation
of the god of withheld
Poetry.

The inauguration of nasty

I'm looking for a bar with young people
who can reduce my experience of this bar
to everything that is not this bar.

Welshpool bunny boiler sells me 20£ of beer
but don't look at me
or Janet.

The essential drama is—one suffers without conflict
because.
Leave me alone with—

Young people lie
as marvellously leaving a room.
Biographies trail begrudgingly after vitality.

I am young I know it as a smell
as a sky which raises death above time.

Below, dancers, walkers, thinkers
HUMAN PARTICIPATION
that Nivea scent.

Any experience is historical
which asks to be believed.

Janet left Burger King 3 weeks ago.
Every night she drinks and laughs, a little
man skirts about her like Monday,

in pink, white, and blue—
These are flowers, not colours.

Believe me or tell me you do,
just don't look for the description
of a certain place,
a man of a certain bed,

a seduction for which you could have paid less
and still do.

In a day

Daylily
we practice
wanting beyond
what we know

or

knowing
beyond wanting
what the other is

NIGHT

We are moody
        chestnut shells   in bed
lessened by   love you   pills
        dream of paralyzed girl who steps
on your chest with stilettos, sexy, on

Jealous   o'clock   turn (still in bed)
but flying out soon
          thumb over my breast   eyelash
    moon
               this in June

One day man will have 6 fingers
I will have a hotter walk

Why I cannot say

I'll be   moonlit   delivery,
              pizza man waning in the brilliance
              of the unknowable woman
              parked car   piss   there   OK
              at my window I don't see any of this

Your reflection, walrus object, my favourite animal
All it does is tickle itself

Tickling is the catastrophe of getting what you want
so thoroughly it's funny. Let's take each other seriously.

Arrowed light divides love and like

                    I speak to those who already understand me

There are rooms for this. There are vastnesses   later
further

IN THE ROOM WHERE IT CAN BE SAID
THE MEETING TAKES PLACE

Almost April

I telepathized *eyelid*
You said *Iranians in Thailand*
I'm a snitch for you

I would prefer separate houses   one pool
          two jackets each   at least you
          not so many more than me   so I want more
jackets, also to eat on your desk   not mine

I am yours as much as you're in mine,
lured out of each to the other is closeness,
glare-glazed   sour me
correctly,   gayly

Cover to cover
a wide full fact   of yellow

Two olives at dusk
as much an ocean, darkly,
a beast in prayer

Beauty is its tender ruthlessness

At the laundry we drink a can
I read Angel's laundromat
You look for estate-sale auction items
I like your new hobby

It's the day before the first day of spring
Toward yesterday
toward his brother

I wash your jeans
in the deliciousness of this dusk

To take them off
is Pruning the Miracle,
is the full grace of fact

steadily to what is
from what is not.

DAYS

1 breast blanket hospital
  plexiglass
2 father's watch grandma's
  brooch mother's cheek
3 carseat pacifier rubber
  conscious milk
4 diaper touches me then I
  try
5 grandmother's shoulder edge
  of crib
6 water faucet plug
7 mine own cheek
8 mine hind leg
9 wetness of my cry
10 my cheek wet too

```
100 toy
111 metal bed frame
130 teeth
140 suckable chin
365 mine own lever the
    beginnings of my first
    tooth
366 confetti cartilage
402 carriage juice
509 apricot fuzz
```

```
1007 feather
2002 ponytail
3652 rubber flipper sole
4100 report card boob
5734 first job joke cheque
6205 rolled up bill
6207 tampon twist in dairy
     queen
6232 portable summer on
     slackened bed
6300 acid manicure place
7651 japanese lantern hand in
     hand crush wrist too
```

```
8071 indisputably purple
     grape
8132 adult laundry basement
     geyser at dawn
     pisco sour at D's home
9643 shed tears
10220 starlingbone
11452 egocling
23901 in the jailsweat of
      racked selves
      thirst trap which
      collects
```

Aphorisms in that fact

I with shrine.
Wading I to me.
I ugly strangers. Yawn.
I all lovemaking
Except tomorrow
I would.

However good behind flesh
Gather with wisdom.

I'll wet
nor speak name

A A A A

If is life
Ask the living.

What shining to God
Forget highest money.

Let blinds of everywhere's matter be days.
Everything bodies.
I without what hunger required
more
the thing outside,

I with sunlight part.

Belief travels to discernment,
tugging wide to meet full friend
without the without half to my lament.
Let give
In yesterday's robe.

Give nearness
amid teeth.

You Held of
nameless
turned from fake.
Randy mentioned
by me.

Life's cock sorry,
I learning showered.
I is how my load as me
I felt, the guy.

Stamps no one can rip off my flesh

Gather the Albanian Cinderellas
under the Duomo—injured simply
but game over.
Hotel check in—nightfall
blindfolded
because a country ends
so the alphabet.

I remember to call you in the noisy fire,
the difference between noise and smoke
they said was listening,
fearful bodies just smell
of fernet and raki and sand.
Specifically when I'm tired
I love the end.

Be like simply

Be a bullet
through Thursday

Be an airport
you said was trust

Write me, call me back,
the envelope—
in the heat—
yellow tree—
no longer tourists—

Babylonian graffiti—
stone chandelier on my back
the choir seduced syllables
into envelopes
and altar silence—

Write me, call me back
I know somewhere I am mentioned
by dull kitchen knife.

The end

is a terrible fool

is a shadow

comes down

on the grin
of every step

takes the night off
every first love

the end is without friend
without quality

pinned to a cloud
it's the full bleating sky

the flight attendant
asks for rubbish

clocks swell to
10

over Saskatchewan
Ocean.

It's the end.

If I'm flesh then you're that other part

1

The jinkl'd kiss hanging off the halfbed
was so banned
the great big laugh
into the vaster set,
desire without master—
of criminals,
adolescents.

You are an adolescent,
I your much older lover.

All your being here
beats inside me.

I float in your ancient wisdom.
You have the oldest eyes.

I can't unsee myself
with you.

So good could
rest forever on that mouth.

In the drinkable darkness
I think I loved you.

2

Hope is vain,
flee the temple
before it's too pleased with your lament.
Let clouds soak up the milk.
Only outside your body
can you live.

3

Since I heard about you
I wanted to get your book.
The library is empty,
another has your book.
That person,
whoever she may be,
is reading you.
I am thinking about you,
all the reasons
I must read you.
I would like to be close to you.
You're a mystery to me.
What good is it to you now
I wonder.

To existing so stone

Love to work so I did
Loved parts across this discipline
Love I almost faked but might come
here veils vatic what chosen love to
requires his from whom all hear "rejection"
writing up in philosopher's terms:
"there's Ami"
to existing so stone

You sensed aliveness in me so came
[the spectrum of a trumpet playing D4]
the song behind his forehead sensed by the ants at his feet
in eyes this example speaks behind promise
as is small in poems to whom is ready
to existing so stone

Return my centuries, my words
to me

Forehead man,
leave my eruption alone

To birds at the end of his adolescence

He owes you money.

In your language,
here is a bum leaning against a tree
with one eye closed.

Mursel—lessons!
Shejtan—lessons!
Bejram—lessons!

Three lessons on the science of laziness.
So tried, the fig falls into his mouth!

Ottoman modestly
makes Osman honest
but naughty dreams
self-accuse a man—so
the dink
of ice cubes in a glass.

He doesn't have any money
No cash
No Spanish money
No coins

Forget conversations with God
Forget daydreams in hotel lobbies
Forget abortions in July
Forget counting queens who arrive

All day he unfleshes the stone
to get to the weakness under its robe.
A purse of birds falls—

The wind decides to which we will refer.
The unemployed seldom are as jobless
as we think.

Here is the warrior of skin
slurping moonshine,
taking it all in.

A think interrupts his
yawning into Rome.

An abandoned cloud
floats out
alone,

is eventually too
the aging
deathless
snow.

Nothing goes into the dark trees to vanish

Nothing is lovelier than sunlight upon teeth
or the plaincloth'd yes in that poor ugly organ:
the mouth.

Tongues of not are no less lovely
than'th'yawn I do and she does:

> *Yes into islandlike oneness*
>   into the lull of the centre

> *Yes the palm of the opening*
>   the dream of your mother

> *Yes the roar in her sleeping*
>   the phone from the kitchen

> *Yes the pubescent claim*
>   of things emanating from the core

> *Yes the lone grass quiver.*
>   Tremble, timekeep,

>   Maybe rain.

I want to want you

in a fraternal moment

like a giraffe's neck
in search of a head

I want to want you so bad
in those things you are
that you are
you are

I want to be your groom
your helmet-brained coach kin

I'm that sorriness
in your bad guitar

I'm that notebook
you wish could drive

through all my wanting
like a shield

but my wanting wants your
crumb's delight

without a place to yell from
like that night when the moon
hung our clothes on the line

and we flew into it a single
dragonfly

I had only dawn to laugh into
along the yellow years of happy
from your neck

Here—I can't give them back
or make memory metaphor

April blooms jasmine
and the sea has its friends

Neighbours

In the elevator
he sulked
as she entered.

He is balding a little
but presentable.

Her ponytail curls
at the end.

In the purr of slow revelation,
a shallow boredom meets hollow patience:
an interminable hello.

12 floors of silence
which make up
years.

The gained floors
pool into everywhere's
armpit,

into the reaching distance,
1000 unreachable goodbyes.

I could have had a better time

Traded for a bigger loan,
played a simpler game.
I could have come early,
made stranger songs
while I waited for you in the stairway.

I could have been my father's boy:
tempted demon, lonely heir,
death befalls the chaperone
taking young girls to his mouth.

My confessed self
to my own self speaks:
You all pack knives,
each conceding, nodding,
each with a wallet that opens in the middle.

All you ringers died in love,
lukewarm with a backache
you take medication for.

I take my clothes off after you sleep,
you haughty-breath't toads
nudie-dancing against my teeth,
yelling for your enema,
but on the wrong end!

I press on, unevenly,
the endured encounter,
on your chest I kneel to piss
on a qualifying patronym.

I am a happy washbowl
of split hairs.
I am the beachcomber
wading across reeds
in red and green blazes.

I could have had a better time,
but cool clutters the will
as time bends to a crescent,
disappearing.

Water spends itself
like laughter
making words with shadows,
keeping hours blue
under its belt.

Institutes

the path of a whistle through a foggy night

charged
fanatic

everything has language
nothing speaks

I hear your video through your headphones

whisper through
foggy path

how many images can I make from shadows

I'd clean the house to avoid it

I'm so tired today
I could do anything here

terrible sleep
too much energy

check sink for cockroaches
one is bound there
by onion skin

shortcut ordinary methods
pasta
Gisele Bündchen does not eat tomatoes

a whistle travels through fog
a whisper shuns the teeth

envelope in a car
with a tiny piece of paper inside

something about the path that's happier
looking straight onto the man who walks it
and his happiness growing
the less he looks

March 1998

They packed. They unpacked. They misplaced nothing.
The crowd at the ferry wore grey wool—
Tiger-faced men and
women embalmed with agony
stand in line
while I wait
inside my mother.
Voices grow closer to bodies.
Scream in a scream
in a chest.
In Greece—we whispered on the bus, got baptized, chose
    pseudonyms.
I was 6 when I shat myself in Kypselis at the basement
    window.
I recited my first poem then.
Princess Diana died that month.
Quiet on the bus.
Dying is part of it.
When life refuses,
the mouth widens.
It could hold
a country
inside
it.

Two photographs

I showered
I dusted
I am without illusions
I've left me alone

Dust settles
taking up yesterday's space

What is yesterday in a poem

What is beauty but sun
for the common is often lovely and unpraised

Someone slept here the night before
Change those pillowcases and sleep opposite, feet to head
At the end of her life, she yelled
Turn me! Turn me!
She says the sunrise means no thing.
Night and day: *turn me! turn me!*
Now I wear this gold
all this gold on my wrist
all this gold on my ears
all this gold on my fingers
The sunrise—
it doesn't capture a thing.

Your name is dearer to me
than what is perfectly true
so I call out from under here.

Don't learn more words he says.

This summer he died and the summer after she followed.

We were translating a transcript from the other bed:

Përzhitje	digestion
Përzjerje	mixture
Ngatëresë	mess
Djersë e mëditsve ne fabrikë	sweat of the factory workers
Për në salle të kinemasë	in the cinema
Vari / Vargë / Vargje	Grave / Range / Verse

The actor forgets his role
His eyes closed under the
shower of a Mexican motel

End

Burg, fabrikë ose Meksikë

Përndjekje – e kupton
përndjekjen?

The thing which comes
after the other thing
End
Either follows or chases

What is the difference?

Chasing is faster than
following

Xhelatë jetimorësh

the man who beats orphans
the fascist fiancée

Gjini federuar

[   ]

Për jetë a vdekje

For Life or death
Death or life
Ask your uncle

What time is it?

11:30

Bring me the second half so
I'll be hungry for dinner

As long as we have strength
we continue

I told her to eat to be strong, but this word also means power
where I'm from
and power looks upon life blindly.

I will never see her sitting there again I say,
but who am I and what's there?

In one photograph,
I'm on your breast having eaten,
tugging slightly on his shirt
your hand on my knee,
crooked smile,
eyebrows ribbons.
You took pride in your appearance.
I can't imagine you in this room now
but there is a desk against the door.

In another,
hand slightly tucked into coat jacket,
rolling your tongue along the sides of your mouth,
you didn't listen to music.
I don't know if you liked it,
I never asked you.
I don't regret it.
I feel all your knowledge inside me
but what to do with it?

I heard water has perfect memory
across sky, sea, body.
It rained 14 days straight,
then one week of sun before you went.

I never was so wet,
nor so elegant,
never did I suffer a grief so round:
I lost my childhood,
you lost your death.

Visiting

a banana in my hand
revolts against death
did you care I was alone
did it matter I was dying
having died I handed
that banana your palm
the sun bled
its eyes

cookie crumbles in my palm
my last memory of you was
fingered red
needy like dirt
sweet
ness sicke
ning

actually chewy
see you on Friday
awaiting no one
having eaten nothing
at your house
that was tomorrow
the rest is future

2021-1929
teeth before bowels go
then the waistline dabbles

gravit-ass lovely lass
how I longed to meet
you then
ears noses
continue to grow
in the drama of decay
going felt like
flying
full of guilt

still the banana
in my bag
nags me
wrapped in
napkinned
silence

I didn't call
I expected you to be here
where do you go
at 6 am buying peaches
under tin canopy

voices mottled
skin chlorophyll
rashcool under chin
you let me in
I'm at your house

I'm visiting visiting
still cruel
dog cool

this photo of your husband
wakes me at night
his eyes over my head
pouring life
over me
or agony
the alertness to which
is my legacy

Unavoidably yours

Refer to me as such,

It's the complication of god
the world explains thusly.

I don't want to scare you it's only that
we are all in war with time for love of you.

How to explain, my resty muse—
the menstruating stars are cooking over this city—
why do I lust after the unfelt burn?
why torture me as though the love is unheard?
I heard, I felt, I burned.

Let ends have girls
Let girls have girls

who are lesser women for having been,

like confidence in Germany is a sorry thing.

Refer to me as a chore
or don't speak at all.

Outside your door

with backward eyes,
glad, drunk.

Ugly angels speak to me
through a bell.

They say *go*

but I feel wise
from hanging on.

On the other side you're trying to extend
the infinitesimal into infinity
until actual things.

You like things because you're private
and can attach meanings to them
secretly.

You say you have never really considered
politics and romance equally before

but here I am.

So do you want to see an elegant crawl
under the banner of
Being?

Go from my door, you say
but I cannot.

Go from my window, you say

but I cannot go,
so long
as I'm going.

By going I mean I'm staying.
If I stay I am
and am not

going.

I cannot go

I is already
the stuff in you

and going is
the waiting room
of the recruited.

Let's

This breath against you ran
sheathing toughness
from beaten lung.

Unbring your message.
Undo your sign.

My little palm—
Rub you, you say,
to be more strong.

My langly plum—
Tickle you, you say,
to keep you still.

The night is earless.
The night is dumb.

Give me that happy question
from your sleepy tongue.

NOTES

In a day: The line "beauty is its tender ruthlessness" is from Alice Notley's *Song for the Unborn Second Baby* (Distance No Object, 2021). "Angel's Laundromat" is a short story by Lucia Berlin from *A Manual for Cleaning Women* (Picador, 2016).

Unavoidably yours: The line "we are all in war with time for love of you" is a reference to Shakespeare's sonnet XV.

Woods: The italicized lines are from Witold Gombrowicz's *Cosmos* (Yale University Press, 2005, p. 68).

Institutes: The end is my mistranslation from Maurice Blanchot's *L'arrêt de mort* (Gallimard, 1948, p. 30), which reads, *"Malheur au sentier qui se retourne pour dévisager le passant; et combien plus profond était ce malheur, combien plus ignoré et plus silencieux."*

Two photographs: *A transcript from the other bed (Transkript nga krevati tjetër,* Onufri, 2020) is the title of a book by Albanian poet Ervin Hatibi. The poem "Come closer" borrows its three opening lines from my translation of the Hatibi poem *"Afrohu"*.

ACKNOWLEDGEMENTS

Thanks to the editors of the publications in which some of these poems first appeared, some in earlier versions: *Commo, Contemporary Verse 2, HELD Magazine, Pinhole Poetry, Rejected Lit, Shrapnel, The Ex-Puritan, University College Review,* and *Who do you think you are: a journal of autotheory.*

Thanks to Connie McParland, Michael Mirolla, Anna Van Valkenburg, and Dylan Curran. Thank you to Rafael Chimicatti for the cover and interior design. Thanks to my editor, Elana Wolff, for her guidance.

Thanks to Benjamin de Boer, Yoyo Comay, Nicholas Hauck, Eddy Wang and Fan Wu for exploding what language can do. Thank you to Parastoo Anoushahpour, Christophe Barbeau, Ryan Ferko, Ben Meyerson, Adam Cavanaugh, Toleen Tous, Mabshid Rafici for listening to earlier drafts. Thanks to Felix Kalmenson for titular ideation.
Thank you to Maria Bun and Rupali Morzaria for their sustained support and enthusiasm. Thanks to Ray Tran and his photographic vision. Thank you to Ted Rawson for his magic.

Thanks to Mia Xherro for her wisdom and to my parents, Eva and Vaso Xherro, for teaching me perseverance.

Thanks to Faraz Anoushahpour in his Neptune years for total love and radical acceptance.

Thank you to everyone for whom these poems are for.

ABOUT THE AUTHOR

Ami Xherro is a poet. She performs with the Toronto Experimental Translation Collective, co-edits *Barricade: A Journal of Antifascism & Translation*, and is a graduate student at the University of Toronto's Centre for Comparative Literature. *Drank, Recruited* is her first book.

MIX
Paper
FSC® C100212
www.fsc.org

Printed in April 2023
by Gauvin Press,
Gatineau, Québec